TERRIFIC MELANCHOLY

Roddy Lumsden's first book *Yeah Yeah Yeah* (1997) was shortlisted for Forward and Saltire prizes. His second collection *The Book of Love* (2000), a Poetry Book Society Choice, was shortlisted for the T.S. Eliot Prize. *Mischief Night: New & Selected Poems* (Bloodaxe Books, 2004) was a Poetry Book Society Recommendation. His latest collections are *Third Wish Wasted* (2009) and *Terrific Melancholy* (2011). His anthology *Identity Parade: new British and Irish poets* was published by Bloodaxe Books in 2010.

He is a freelance writer and editor, specialising in quizzes and word puzzles, and has held several residencies, including ones with the City of Aberdeen, St Andrews Bay Hotel, and as "poet-in-residence" to the music industry when he co-wrote *The Message*, a book on poetry and pop music (Poetry Society, 1999). His other books include *Vitamin Q: a temple of trivia lists and curious words* (Chambers Harrap, 2004). In 2009, the Poetry Foundation awarded him the Bess Hokin Prize. He is poetry editor for Salt Publishing. Born in St Andrews, he lived in Edinburgh before moving to London.

RODDY LUMSDEN

Terrific
Melancholy

BLOODAXE BOOKS

ISBN: 978 1 85224 908 3

First published 2011 by
Bloodaxe Books Ltd,
Highgreen,
Tarset,
Northumberland NE48 1RP.

www.bloodaxebooks.com
For further information about Bloodaxe titles
please visit our website or write to
the above address for a catalogue.

Supported by
**ARTS COUNCIL
ENGLAND**

Cover design: Neil Astley & Pamela Robertson-Pearce.

Printed in Great Britain by
Bell & Bain Limited, Glasgow, Scotland.

i.m. Craig Arnold (1967-2009)

and

i.m. Paul Reekie (1962-2010)

ACKNOWLEDGEMENTS

Acknowledgements are due to the following publications and websites where some of the poems were published: *By Grand Central Station We Sat Down and Wept* (Red Squirrel, 2011), *Fuselit*, *Headshook* (Hachette, 2009), *Ink, Sweat and Tears*, *Magma*, *The Manhattan Review*, *The Moth*, *Night and Day*, *Poetry*, *Rhino*, *Rising* and *Tall-Lighthouse Review*.

'What the Shrimp Calls Its Tail I Call Its Handle' was commissioned by the BFI for the Psychopoetica project. Many thanks to The Poetry Foundation for the award of the 2009 Bess Hokin Prize and to Dominic Frain for patronage which allowed me to travel and write.

Thanks to A.B. Jackson and Ahren Warner for their helpful advice on the manuscript.

CONTENTS

FROM THE GRAVE TO THE CRADLE

Could I pass all words through the end of seeing,
new would rise to speak of working.

SARAH GRIDLEY

Posthumously published. But my father had evident plans for it. Synopses, dozens, handwritten and typed. Specialist presses circled on a xeroxed list. And the notebooks and logbooks, near two hundred of them, dated and stacked on the shelves beneath his extensive fungi library – a side project. Charts and columns where he had regardfully recorded varying falls and patterns of dust within the home and surrounding outbuildings, between the first moon landing and the Cold War's end. Ciphers in blue pen and red. Fine and finer particularities of dusts, their peculiarities and aberrations, lists of their specific names in Sanskrit and the Celtic tongues. Diagrams and drawings and thereafter Polaroids. An essay on the wearing of khaki, which means *dust*, an essay on the history of the abacus, which means *dust* and a tally of all that was found weekly on a tarpaulin stretched in a clearing one mile from the steading but mainly, the view kept close, the micrometer's divinings, a sweep for fragments and filings on the unused kitchen worktop, a licked finger cosseting the length of a tabletop, a welcome mat flipped and shaken above an underlit screen. Eyes tight perhaps, he listened for descent – all things fall – a smut, a granule, a dying fly (those pressed and parched in the logs circled and pet-named, with humour we had never witnessed in our boyhoods). Such elegance of phrase, such turns in which, we must assume, his best self lives on. The first edition was endorsed by poets. I'm told the King of Jordan marvelled at it on his deathbed, making notes as he read, his last word *dust*.

Sakes

All that I said after midnight, disregard.
Except this: it is not that I exist, more
that I am *implied*.

All the talk is of cockroach and sage
as if there aren't ten million creatures
(multiplied by gender)

as which we could return: sea lion bull,
Argentine blue-bill drake, melon thrip,
maybe tax collector.

This time of waiting barely hurts –
like the first months of love, it zooms by:
chemical and queasy.

For ease, we call ourselves *sakes*.
And, talking soft, we call this place *limbo*,
there being no easy

word for the truth of it as, once a minute,
we shuffle up the endless bench, ready
to open our mouths wide.

The World

when I return will roll blue and gold

the gone restored in niches   set and measured

where soft flaws flourish   lead flaws flag

a kin unbowed by traits   all at a taking age

no sleeveless errands   no call for alibis

unwindowed rooms   a pure song snug in the head

my enemy distilled to a tot   and swallowed

the sauce will be smoky   the ale fierce and cold

the solution   a key in the palm of the hand

dark reason skittled   with animal precision

and I will not fear women   laughter   human touch

the beast asleep on my chest   purring   mild

the land of make do   sunk beneath turning surf

the sweet bath drawn from which I'll rise   hands high

True Crime

We leave our blood in each hotel –
a blot of it enough to tally with
an honest deed, an inquest or a trial.

Reborn from an ear print on a bolster,
a heel scuff on a skirting board,
we cash ourselves in undercover,

turn ourselves in after we have left,
our leaving cited by a drying print
or stray thread picked off in the lift.

We leak and melt and peel, losses
compensated for, blood money
paid in notes to self, good guesses

made by golems, fetches, clones
who'll stride on where we were,
their pockets hard with foreign coins.

Many go missing – but none *are* lost.
Misfortune knows that. Each bridge
should name the river it has crossed.

The Shilling Hotel

Though the centenarian had a room,
she played the days through
in a corner of the street level fry bar,

spinning out a few stewed, milky teas,
a butterless chicken sandwich
and stared into what was off-stage

for the rest of us, at what we assumed
was the swishing life she'd led
but was, in truth, less than nothing much.

Nights, we'd see her through the blind –
too gone to stir from her freeze, still
as beef – expect each morning to find her

tilted cold and open-jawed. Yet each time,
she returned, less *from* compelling death,
more *into* each next, each necessary life,

just as a clamberer over ice is sucked
by black charm towards a place
where to fall and die seems the only choice

and holds that thrill – inhuman lack –
and pivots between trust and will
then heels back onto the gifted path.

Yeast

A word you can't quite say
without itching, flinching; it's not easy
to ignore its squirming appetite, stay
your primal juddering. And yes, at
night, each microbe gurns in the salty sea
of gut and gullet, born again, boldly eats
as you ate it, brews its own queasy tea
of proto-raunch which it will quickly sate,
birthing wanderlusting vigours, as yet
unknown to microscience. They sashay, set
out for the toes or gape through your eyes at
your drooping lids, your fat bunch of keys, at
this internal motel's boss, bellhop, lackey, sat
in the throne of his slumber, a mercy seat.

And Back Again

One bad thread and all comes loose. But never has.
And look, you're wearing red on such a day, an XXL day,
your anklet tattoo a mistake, right there at the foot

of Christmas Steps, a place I'd never been but knew
in an instant, from a better life; they say these steps
have topped and tailed with Russian sailors, that

knifesmiths cutled and cranked in the backways, that
the lost choruses of carousers from the Bacchus
and nine more pubs rumped in the Bristol Blitz

still peal here and that, each dawn, a ghost kitten pegs –
and back again – four feet above the slabs. And this
the becoming season when need needs its acre, each

memory arriving more sinuous than the last (*one bad
thread*) and you already lost in one, impermanent,
inaccurate, in red, walked west toward the water.

What I say of my enemy: he couldn't spot a pretty girl
on Park Street; what I say of my ally: he thrives
like wild violets thrive on There and Back Lane.

Ceremonial

Bleak cherries fall through bleak leaves of the bleakest tree.
You are in their pillow talk   as a loaf stands in a pantry.

A glitch of silver shies along a whet, or roams a coil of steel.
You are mentioned in their papers   as a bone juts in a tail.

Fresh quiet dips on all the chessboards along the promenades.
You are whispered of then   as the next life is in this.

No one can tell how far away a light is out there on the ocean.
You are in their will   as soft   often means uneven.

Command to Forget

You arrive equal, in the manner of most beasts
and then begins the extrication, a classical
diagnosis; prepare to be sifted for gold-specks.

All the lives lived, all the devilish spurnings,
the haywire of secrets, the kelp of shame and
thoughts no man should have in bible hours.

You were no mere skimming, no off-scouring,
not a sweeping, but nor did you equal a star;
you're a trimming, a peg in the chronicle's bag.

All the palaces of small mercies pillaged;
in the ruins wags a book of wiving strategies,
the new skin skidding round the old chicanes.

You would dally, but it's not the destination
that matters, not the journey, but the arrival:
the past has sickened you; the future's a trap.

All those wounds and woundings, drolleries
of the unborn, apostolic effigy, carbon copy
threats, all the clipped ransom notes to self.

You make a fist at the falling of a beech leaf,
grit your teeth at the neap tide's minor daring,
sciamachist by the wall of what went before.

All the lights fussed up – flint and bow drill,
iliou persis, Pharos, Menlo Park; great works
mouthed on grey terraces, on bright avenues.

*

18

You're thrown into the machines of repetition:
now the treadmill begs your cipher of authority
as once the *shaduf* requested your endless song.

And folly becomes folly's intuitive colour
and the *azif* perpetuates the nighttime desert,
its annals in ravenous, sulphurous bigtime.

You dip into the herd's maw, fearing being
snagged in the bringdown. Implacable ontrot,
the individual lost to the roving mechanism.

All these starlight pourings through stigmata;
what is their history is our arcana, our cant,
our winking chintz; our sob story is their lore.

You note a stream's century vacation of an inch,
you scree ride, carry boulders on head for miles
for wagers; you loosen scrimshaw from a bone.

All the loved fields behind bartons and all
the misgivings, the nimbling, the cuss, dates
uncircled, scotomata yawning in calendars.

Your repertoire was wame sang and cork-pop,
serenade and yearn. You plan your comeback,
fear for torch song, katzenjammer, threnody.

And in the duked outskirts, slates split keen.
And appetite whets each canine and seedclaw
and the runes clatter in chance's showdown.

*

You return, your trail blazed by the cynosure
of significance then error, significance, error,
coxswained along that evercoasting river.

All the skew. All the scanning from heights,
the fleeing, the flea bites. All the wrenched
choices of mothers, star counts, migrations.

You marry the tideline – your last clothes hang
drowsy on you – then round the lake's brink
unobserved, as a girl in morning's chorus.

And the knitted smiles. And a shifting frontier
mapped by downfalls, and sour fumes which
cloak the earth, tempting embers in the chaff.

You court the slopes where mist-fed trees are
dripping; your eyes wind to where a lily pad
surfaces. The sluggish bristlecone outlives us.

All the tiny earlies: creeping myrtle, creeping
phlox and squill rolling back in tidal duty.
All the nubbins. All the velvety advancers.

You step through the slats of the sunshower,
down to the lip of the ooze, where mouths
break the surface: breath, the origin of truth.

And you are your own wealth, well spent.
And you accept now the command to forget:
body a spun token, name a bell new-sounded.

Alsace

Six months into life, inch-close to pasture,
the hen pheasant tilts her marmalade eye
to this sweet, fallen seed – a jewel match.

Forgotten now the past life bill of torture,
a rock python's grip, a silver bag skyed
into squealing traffic, the gunpoint march.

Bowdler in Heaven

One hand is lost in the mane of Aslan,
the other fingering a virgin cocktail,
his appearance settled somewhere between
child and adult, as all are in the afterwards.

On his lap rests the latest book to bother him,
for its silky pages are odourless, and not
a hint of teachery, not a glint of blood
sulks within the tale, and no one dies or hugs.

No need to staunch a cut here or wipe at a stain.
All is iceberg sweet, unalloyed, harm on hold.
He longs for curious things: to wipe his feet
on a doormat, to fret a flea-bite, witness a duel,

yearns for Gretel's squealing, Boccaccio's abbot,
a necronomicon sneaked beneath his pillow.
If he dreams, he dreams of an eye gouged out
or a spill-breasted milkmaid touching her toes.

For we are what we are on earth and know it
as sure as the lusty boy who asks his mother,
Are we animals? though he already knows it true
and asks again just for the dirty thrill of it.

HAIR AND BEAUTY

Downtown

That's it, you said, that's where it happens, there, and you point
and I look out at the old Lincolns sliding past Izzy
and his shoes sliding past Evo's and Cazelli's.

CHRIS EMERY

There! And the cab slows and some turned to look and just past
the lunch shop, over by the brown bins, squeeze through and win
your way, here's where the cash burns and where the door is
daubed in mustard, behind the pull chains, where the kitten walks,
where Patsy blew once blue his cornet, and if the plaque says
'here lived and died' then *so close*, look for the roaches playing
chicken between curb and doorway, just there, that's it, you can
smell linen and brogues from way back, hear the scissors of
Schmitz the snipper, spot roguing women, you'll know it, in the
shadow of the kitsch mart, in the shade of ten lindens, keen click
of checkers, doorbells, yes, you now know why, here, where lean
men lean, where kids shout for one hour more, before Hanoi
Emperor, after Hammond's you said, and past The Calamity
Belle, there where chauffeurs idle, chrome shine, take a left, but
veer don't spin a ninety, step over sleepers, voguing dogs, hitch
your shoulders, feel the latte draught from the book store, closer,
that's it, at the scent of clove, armada skirt sailing a moment,
wrench of patchouli, clearing house, dollar corner, campaign HQ,
radio zoning between hip-hop, static and prayers, look now, ticket
split ready, wallet thick, tie straight if tie on, part of the pride,
welling, sure, on Saturday, any day, promise of centuries yielding
to promise of rain, you said, borderline wage, half of a soda, wires,
wires, dim sum and impertinent caprice, a whipped sheet just as
good as a flag, mister, here you are, now you are.

The Crown

The Heath, the Village, Tranquil Vale,
the home stretch of the Terrace
and the sun a decommissioned weapon.

Cider, praline, pastilles, gifts for home
this fluthered king presents, some
foisoned patron saint of patience

bearing intention, ungrace, igniting
tinctures sunk at The Crown,
weaving under sacks of consequence,

wearing a crown of skull, scalp, hair
and hat, a crown of winter bite
then night sky's *hug-me* mercy flirt.

El Sombrero de los Reyes

And if I wear a crown of wrong,
it will demand a brilliance of the song
you've known since birth and whistled all along.

Or if I wear a crown of wire,
it teases out your spasming desire
and tots how far you'll spill your scam of fire.

And if I wear a crown of ice,
it will exact a tithing sacrifice
of onions, cream and apple flesh and rice.

Or if I wear a crown of sighs,
I'd summon pout and smudge of alibis
to prove a secret spoken is a lie.

Or if I wear a crown of lightning,
the light I would allow would be inviting
the ladderwork of rumour, clue and sighting.

And if I wear a crown of brine
bespeaking tack and brack, I'd tightly line
you up as saline, silt and serpentine.

So I will wear a crown of crowns
and promenade the borderlands and bounds
of my domains: sad aftermaths, slow towns.

Square One

Going steadily, rowed out from east to west, concrete
gondolas brink the Thames, which is *still* – it's the land which is
googled by gravity, thrown round – an optical illusion
good enough to fool the city's multiplicity of fools:
goons and gomerils who labour under Mammon's lash,
gowks and golems who queue to flash their lips and lids in
god-forsaken church halls, reeking basements and seeping
Golgothas, clamped blithe to ardour: the emos, indie kids,
Goths and ravers melting down the day we launched with
gongs struck in gentlemen's clubs, skirted girls at Nonsuch and
Godolphin thronging in corridors, dawn trains given the
go-ahead at suburban junctions, the first trace of the sun's
gold tide as it washes back to our side of the sphere, but now,

going for lunch, you swing between delight and throwaway,
gourmet and grease, dither between syrah in a silver
goblet or Tizer from a sprung can; you might stare over roasted
goose at the Gay Hussar, at your companion's bowl of
goulash, as retired politicians two tables over whisper scandals,
gossip through dumplings and meggyleves, hissing the latest
Gordon or Boris anecdote, Obama's honeymoon months,
government soap; you might stare at bangers and bubble, tea
gone cold; evening settles in at Kilburn, down Battersea Park;
Golders Green wanes; high-rises throw slant shadows over
Gospel Oak; students breathe the soot of a bendy revving on
Gower Street; in the doorways of basement strip joints,
gorillas strike stances; toms swap fat packs of Fetherlite and

Gossamer, hitch into their tangas and fishnets waiting for the
gonk to finger a phone box card, the way a kid fingers what he
got from the kitchen drawer; evening touches Camden where
gonzos sup Stella; dancers shift in the wings of the opera;
goluptious girls slip into slingbacks, swim into creamy
gowns, or swash out of them, as that misted moon plays
go-between in a city of secrets, crimson or bilious – what
good will become of us, falling in the dark, our names
gouged into plane trees? – we are becoming history,

godmothers to our own torn myths: twisted and crazed,
gorgeous giants, we hang spinning over the still river:
Go on! it murmurs – *own torn myths* – and midnight mentions
Gog and Magog – sweet, towering boys, long gone.

Europe After the Rain

A possible sin: negotiated peace.
A newly off-duty judge plays a piano,
only on the black keys. The stopgap cab
waits in its stall; you can intuit steam,
silt, soot, any gestural substance.

Honey, the only food which never
rots, lights a pantry with its old glow.
The seamstress works alone, even linen
makes her shrug while the most of us
shiver at its imposterous thrill-feel.

A good man now need not be, say,
honest, rippling. The bank notes turn
magenta, vermillion, cyan, poets' shades
and are pulled from long wallets, lit
and burned: flags, fears, apologies.

The photographer seeks the single
one who has not longed to strip and
wade out, beneath the sea. And for now,
Europe exists as quiet terraces, back
rooms where inner oceans moan.

Through a Raised Glass

One thousand thank yous, poet, for telling me
about my own people, for instructing me
in the anthropology of ruder ways
and simplest faiths. I am richer now for gazing
at your word-paintings of the ungrandeur
of the schemes, the base calm of terraces
which hide stout garden sheds scented with
Maxwell House and thinners, where stony men
suck smokes and spin the handle of their vice,
rolled-up tabloids jammed into the rule sleeve
of their overalls. I had never before noticed
the dods of dog dirt on the black bags piled
behind the one-room library, the sick mist
rolling between tower blocks; I was blind
to frozen food palaces on two-Greggs-streets,
bowling halls and bowling greens and bowl-cut
kids whose only sports, I see now, are daydreams
and venom. Had you not veered into the badlands
en route to your office at the end of a corridor,
your cafetière, your modest photocopy budget,
had you not rummaged through the crumpled snaps
of the relatives your family rarely mention,
had you foresworn that commission at the prison
which funded the long weekend in Salamanca,
I would be still be miscueing, hitting the wire,
sending the rain-soaked ball over the crossbar
of the truth, my education being comprehensive
only in name. I would barely recognise myself.

I Will Not Marry You

                              because I frighten easily
because I was born once bitten   unready for love
and because your head is too small for your body
and your nose *somewhat* big for your face
and because when you speak a touch of Quechua
all the brown eyes in the street roll sideways
because you could throw a six at will
making me feel like a wasp on sellotape

and because your hanging baskets are too yellow
because you are less than galsy
because together we'd write the book on studied idiocy
and because your breasts are cobwebby piglets
because I keep warm by hugging a room's corners
and because my ankles are rusted Meccano
because you seem the tenth Muse
whose sisters keep all too quiet about her

because my inner puritan still hisses
because when you point out your enemies
I sweat like a ram in a rainstorm
because you employ words out of context
    anaesthesia   dovetail   drumlin
and because I own no suit for you to sneer at
because on your good days you are halfway
to razzamatazz   halfway to Ragnarök

because my head is a dead weight
with *1 TON* chalked on its dark side
and your throat is the difference in meaning
between *systemic* and *systematic*
because when I try to say *racecar*
the word *camel* drops from my mouth
and because you write in that thick book of yours
because fame has barely heard us mentioned

because for you romance is way down a list
beginning *stitching   filing   canoeing*
because of the white doves which bob and call
nectar songs along your vivid shoulders
because I'll learn to dance with someone
steamier

             give me a warring cascade
a pulsing weir   a purring cataract
I'd dance with *her*   I'll marry one like *that*

Olivier

He married eighty-three times, eighty of them in the West End run of *The Good Husband* (by playwright Alexander Morris, who later shot himself and his chocolate Lab – '*une bufe brune*', which survived – in the Place de la Bastille).

He considered calling all his children after the heroines from the novels of Colette, but had only sons. He was born in Andalucia where his father was stationed. His favourite card game was bezique. His favoured wine was best Tokay.

When steak first cost one pound per pound, he noted this in his diary, which he kept 'fastidiously'. He always carried an apple in his left coat pocket, for luck, he said, or a rainy day (which, incidentally, he liked, particularly a monsoon).

At heart, he still considered himself to be plain Mr Oliver, the trainee gunsmith from Folkestone. He collected packs of playing cards and also postcards and he loved to receive them, especially from Mombasa, where he had been born.

He never kept a diary, though he was given one each year by the Quakers. Once, when they found themselves lost on the edge of a town, he told my father: *Look for the church tower, and follow on: there is always an inn near a church.*

Kerouac

According to his mother, *he climbed onto life and could not get off*. Though a scruff, he would scrimp for eau de cologne which, he explained, gave him 'the philosophy vibe'. He had a stutter, but only when uttering his own surname... or yours.

All of his life's pleasures were spent before he turned the age to understand what pleasure was. 6'4", some said he creaked when walking, either to the nearest sunlit street corner where he liked to dally, or to the cinema where he'd gripe at starlets.

Afternoons were his mornings and evenings his afternoons. For boyhood nicknames, he had Johnny and Kipper. Hobos, gangsters and butchers were his heroes. His surname derives from the Breton for 'the road' which does some explaining.

He became disillusioned on realising he *was* disillusioned – which wasn't the Beat way. Fame clung to him like an itchy scab rosette. He bought a car a year. His favourite smells were creosote and the perfume Primitif, its bottle designed by Dalí.

He rose early and came to love his nightmares, as we all do, but not sunlight, which he avoided. When asked his greatest wish, he told a reporter, *I wish my father was still alive, so I could have one last chance to beat that old varmint at chess.*

Interface

a kiss appears in the air
  within a room
or as a button at the neck
      of one known

which buttons one night
to its morning   where
we talk between love
  where   soft

in the light's spilldown
     a kiss is all
but talk   and spills
all   spilled

lightly into the pulse
     radar concision
the concealed heat
  hoaxed   raised

     from its lair
light heat   and pulse
risen in the notch
     between heads

a kiss appears   is air
  endures not as we wish
    as heat in the head
but as light

in the room we lay in
    as light as down
on one known skin
  endures *as wish within*

Duology

Le jeu lugubre – not one of Dalí's lighter pieces:
autoerotic, omnisexual, a spandulous whorl
of heads and hats and hands. Translated
by bottom feeders as *The Lugubrious Game*,
by the enlightened as *Dismal Sport*, the former
sends the arrow close to its quiddity, the latter
pins its haecceity to the canvas.
                              The way we dress
is beyond our determination, gene-gleaned:
one girl looks a fool in a gown, another glides
into the nightlife in a catsuit; one lad squires
in his homodox jerkin, another skives in a flat cap
he knows is a black fib. History's dayjob
is to usher us closer to its shady marquee.
And so we age: easier to love, harder to desire.

Midtown

the woven streets
oh heart, sit still
jackhammer of luck
a lonesome whistle
a flagless flagpole

unrandom numbers
altocumulus heaping
impassioned weather
storage lot wraiths
the battened kiosk

homespun murals
where will we end?
back-alley smoker
dim of a bookstore
the familiar in reruns

memory of air
rumour of charisma
leeway turns jeopardy
an irenic salute
two rusty terriers

charge of disinterest
was I ever simple?
supernal scotoma
haphazard kismet
a bird's a bird shadow

bonsai, napkin rings
brash urban fauna
treading day's water
her ungiven swirl
past tense as future

The Sign of O

Stranger than this? Arcana only: that which
happens only where the grand waves carry to,
where night falls quick as the warm rain
and life is guesswork, death mediocre to us
in lands we'd misspell, as far wars purr;
nothing that can be blown by the wind
is ever precise and our sightlines follow
this stream we drink from.
                                    Make the sign
of an O and it might bespeak treachery,
might announce love. Arcana, knowing
what's buried and where, the bushman's
honour word, or deciphering the yawns
of the illuminati, by which they exchange
the acumen of the shared judiciaries.

That which lurks, fangtooth and coffinfish,
in the ink of the ocean; that which dallies
at the selvage of our apprehension, blinking
seldom, as the Titan arum lily blooms;
that which slurs below our understanding,
a minnow slowed in the ice, miracle secrets
rashing in minuscule lichen, hope asleep in
a kernel: far stranger than these is what we have,
o far stranger who knows me, colludes me.
We are not hopeless who do not know hope.

The Accumulation of Small Acts of Accumulation

Hours, minutes. The smiles which women
save for children.   The plot left open.
Swallow leagues, chasm inches. Rain in
mid-air. Wedding favours. Pepper flakes.
Brown-cornered pages of torn paperbacks.
The systems of abandon. Toes, toothpicks.

Ambitions dealt face up. Full stops. Thrips.
Maids of dishonour, milk teeth, bottletops.
Bubbles in pumice or weir.   Wire-knots.
Mongrel days. Rags and sparrows. Roof tiles,
ball bearings, whetted nails. Tight coils
of hair. Cowries knocking. Snow quills.

Rivets. Coffins. Frays. A sigh then silence.
Cat's eyes. Mothers and bezoars. Always
divided by always again. Tumbled starlings.
Small change. Surf churn. Small changes.
Hormonal kites sent up.   Half-chances.
Hopes, summers, sad rooms. Beads, hinges.

People, Their Wretchedness

The gatherer of blessings blitzed and bilked
and klutzed and glitched by the doomed day's sulk.

The block squared, best beef cubed, chimneys
huff under rain, bells pine in shop doorways.

The flinty hiss of Shiraz. Null conversation or
retributory showdowns with hazed strangers.

A page corner thumbed to hiatus. In the road,
a one man band of hope, his teaselled head.

Locked gazes of drivers, the ten-count thrill
of whisked skirts. White pills shucked from foil.

Most rooms have no one in them. What slides
down is part water, part grief. A blood tide.

Grit lurks in the honey. Hogtied by glinting relief,
we are our own possible vermin. Vivid meat.

Beelzebub

From this guest bed, in this mood of indolent abjection,
white key melancholy, the door-back coat-hook taunts
and baits with two-prong weaponry and screwhead eyes:
a death's head boosting its fists, an abyssal squid torn
from the black by masked illuminati, a bronze mammoth
charging from the age of spears, a true lord of the flies.
If I had a child, I'd lull him, sweeten the evident dread
we seek in quotidian froth, spin out the last sugar strands
of his innocence. Yet belief too is innocence, that very
seeking being the bleak charm we must allow ourselves
though the flies gather, as they did on the goaty beards
of St Narcissus, in Mother Shipton's wake, and around
the scalp of Miss Hollington as she slugged her last cup
of honeyed tea between bites of marzipan, Satan's paste.

Against Comedy

Sorely drawn to write a poem called 'Art in Heaven',
the tropes and strophes already rolling like pinks
into the corner pockets of quirky perfection, instead
I sit hard on my hands and ponder grander things.

Then, stingingly tempted to rustle up a piece
titled 'When the Saints Go Sitting Down',
a twenty minute job worth a wave of gentle laughter,
I take a long walk without paper, without pen.

You, critic, who claimed me a wit a decade back,
were wrong. My kismet was ultimate profundity
and humour just a stepping stone on which I found
myself, wet-shod, light-hearted, momentarily.

For the museum of high spirits is cold and quiet
while in the palace of pure thought the grim boys
bustle, setting up our nooses and our guillotines
and racks. We aim to make some serious noise.

What the Shrimp Calls Its Tail, I Call Its Handle

Will the truth take your weight? Take your weight when you wonder? And when you wear something fragile and spoilable, drop on some silk or push into lace, who is *en garde*? Not the garment, for that's a bimbo thing, unschooled. Not the designer, her feet up in some loft in Milan, surrendered to a bubble moment. It's you, then, at fault when it all comes apart. Not the poison we should pay blame to, or the poisoner, who tends to have a decent reason, for it's the poisoned ones who are at fault, chilly and retching in a bed of effort, under the cruel eyes of the ward lights, sorry for themselves. And not the trap, laid in long grass so nimbly for noble conclusion; not the stalker (or blunting self) who laid it, an expert in twine, but you, strolling incumbent, with your halo of fate and your foot just one pace away from the steeled jaw of that truth.

The Shuffle

Skipping out from the major international cocktail party
with my becleavaged blight, a jeroboam in her tight fist,
I broke open my copy of *Sarcasm for Beginners*, i.e. men.

Never had I seen so many pairs of to-the-elbow gloves.
Never did I see a puttoed ceiling groan so with thin talk
as the great, the grim and the gone pressed terrible flesh,

so many penguins offering tastesome wisps and skimps
from doilied salvers: cherry-shaded caviar, cheese puffs,
dark sugared berries, dainty octopods, gently vinegared,

with not enough tentacles to count the capes and stoles,
fine bespoke pashminas, silk snoods, at least one vicuna
suit, tainted with gold thread. I'd seen down a Blenheim,

two Lime Rickeys and was eyeing a gamine mixologist
who was straining out Savoy Royales when my raddled
nemesis limped over to announce she had encountered

my latest column, all four foot eleven of her tortoiseishly
quivering, a nubbin of cream cheese on her whiskery lip
and her good eye withering my borrowed companionette

as she leaned on air. I am not a man who has not known
the turmoil women offer, the gift you accept of their wit,
the way you'd slip a hand into a gloveful of cockroaches,

comply with a last minute call to join a seal cull. Tanya,
Tanya, I pouted, I am honoured you opened a window
in your schedule even to glance at my inconsequential

outpourings – at which point she clattered out a scoffing
gibe so sour you couldn't blend it with a chemistry set
from Hamley's and, seizing my escort by her neat wrist,

we tore out onto Jermyn Street, along which I performed
a sort of shuffle, one eye on the book and one on m'lady's
competition-standard backside as she led us to the Ritz.

44

1979

They arrived at the desk of the Hotel Duncan
and Smithed in, twitchy as flea-drummed squirrels.

Her coat was squared and cream, his patent shoes
were little boats you wouldn't put to sea in.

People, not meaning to, write themselves in
to the soap that your life is, rise or fall in the plot.

Seems that they were fleeing from the 1980s
much as a hummingbird flies from a flower's bell.

These were the times when wine was still a treat
and not yet considered a common bodily fluid.

You will have heard that the mind works much
as an oval of soap turned between two hands.

She went round the room seeking lights
that could be off without desire becoming love.

He spread his arms behind his head, a gesture
of libido she misread as test of temperature.

Every carpet has its weave and underlay, seen
only by the maker, the deliverer and the layer.

The year was a dog but the day was as good as
a song that ends with a wedding, meat on the rib.

Evening was folding over the grid, slick walkers
with armfuls of books splendoured in dusk's ask.

The song of the pipes was eerie as a face pressed
to glass, as a basketball with a mouth and teeth.

They lay in the glow of the times and talked of
how people form a queue to exact or escape love.

Each sigh has a sequel, she thought, then he did,
then the whole hotel pulsed through that thought.

Scandal has an in-road, but you must tunnel out;
she rose and stood up counting, all hair and beauty.

Though we do not hear them, beneath our own,
our shadows' footsteps clatter, they match our dread.

Daredevil

*The Scottish crossbill is the only vertebrate unique to the
British Isles and was confirmed as a species in 2006 on the
basis of having a distinctive bird song, a 'Scottish accent'.*

Precarious work, keeping watch on three kestrels
as they scud and lift, patrolling from trough-lip
to paddock-post at Honeydale, seeing through
their evening shift. Yet no sleuth could track
the Scottish crossbill, mazing in a sifting flock
of cousins, or snugged in the innards of a larch
or lodgepole, its zincy chirrup proved unique
by sonograms. Who'd be a namer? Who'd paint
endemic on a door, position the decibel meter,
steep their instruments and slides for the sake
of lethal precision, exacting victory? After years
of triumphs, Knievel only reached the lips of fame
in the wake of a first near-death crash. I wish to be
the captain of the things which have no names.

Ten Things You Ought to Know About the Song Thrush

one   A thrush begins where a struggle has ended
and sweetnesses rise in new grass.

two   The thrush is not a please and thank you bird
and does not resort to laughter.

three   The thrush sits nimbly between *thrum* and *thrust* –
two words he knows no need for.

four   The egg of the thrush is the blue of the water
in the Well of the World's End.

five   When the song thrush meets a violet with one eye,
he meets his most equal.

six   In winter, spark a candle at your smallest window
and a thrush will tarry nearby with his song.

seven   The thinker exalts the thrush, for he runs from
metaphor to metaphor, misease in a coat of allure.

eight   If all the thrushes of the thicket vapourised,
then the world would drift in space.

nine   Once dead, a song thrush can be rolled thin
and used as a map of any downlands.

ten   To remember a thrush, give him a regal name
and pin him to your memory.

Uptown

Dusk sees me reading the lanes between
houses. I sense there is something so
obvious no human has thought of it,
cousin to the colours none of us see, or
to fever, which I have failed to portray.
A thing beyond the laws now unified
and the rules compromised. Beyond
somatic clamber and the seething core.
And it may as well be here, where
patterns lift me and every twelfth step
my sidewise look breathes in these
brief amplitudes, sudden lands where
the seed might fall and flame, with
mower, ashcan, trampoline their twilit
sentries. If one suggests the fuzz of a
quantum *is*, the next translates the
evening into half-song. This seesaw of
thrill and calm presents a concave
mirror where the inner one bulges,
seeking the unrealised device, to untrick,
to unthing. The next lane shows a sky
escaped, the next a crypt where shy
light shies. Barrow, glasshouse and
stacked stones, the webbed and tarry
hatch of a kennel; now the washed light
is tense between cornerhouse taverns,
is birdsong in a cinefilm or else its
celloey tang hints at a physics beyond
us. The unseen might be discerned in
abature and alley, the arcane unmasked
and then clutched in sideways and
vennels. The found thing would sit till
needed behind an ear. It will fit in
cupped hands. The last of day will catch
at it; revolution spills from its shadow.

Terrific Melancholy

We did arrive in this life separately
and I have observed love forming
    its formal, hopeful queue
    close to where you stand.
I would trust my challenge, would lick
your reflection from a dirty window,
    but I have flicked a dozen
    pages forward in the script
and we do not play a scene together
and we will not make a scene together.

*

Twilight rowing with the silver birches
as I rally a list of parts I have played.
    See, I can do this with words:
    no promenade, no costume.
And the apparatus needs no system.
And the apparatus needs no action.
    But some words turn phosphor,
    some are surefire currency.
In this street of words tonight walk
allies, champions, all sweet thieves.

*

And though I am far inland, I hear
desire has a coast. As so do you,
    if I so choose to say so,
    or if I choose to trace you,
counting skerries at your shoulder,
inlets at your hip. I fancy black boats
    sail your coast, crewed
    by sweet-smiled apes
who tug at ropes and climb the mast
to gaze across your pearly belly.

Some roles inspire as others congest
and some are sneezed into hindsight,
    shorn of semblance, torn of
    caprice, a minus sum of parts.
Always some deal about the night.
Always some fuss about some girl.
    They give us an alley to ache in,
    a cliff to hang from, a red barn
where the beast lies beneath a trapdoor
beating the last of love from its hide.

*

I find I am singing a line from a song
from the year you were born: the year
    I was your age. A flashback.
    While on the stage, you play
my (younger) character's (younger) wife
in flashback scenes, I wait, lulling it
    in the wings or dressing room,
    We are the arteries, the vessels
of love, wondering is it the sea that sieves
the stones or the stones that sieve the sea.

*

When I am pretty and still I play
the boy who bites the heads off things,
    a strolling mess of things,
    a cream-faced stripling;
when I must play the pot boy or a ghillie
swashing the heather in a cutaway,
    I count stars, do what I can
    to block the prop lad's yawn,
an inkling this career's a stag in sights,
a melting jigsaw cut from marmalade.

I dream you perfect though your name
is somehow Melba. Then I dream you
    with a whirlpool where
    your mouth should be.
And in all dreams you tell me holy
lies, just as you would, just as I'd play
    a priest as a bull terrier,
    its tongue to the floor,
just as I'd play a whistling suitor,
hungry to flee from the risk of truth.

*

Ten days pass and the crush won't shake;
I lie stunned for nights, supposing justice
    has been shaken, expecting knock
    or knock-on. Ten years might pass
as ten do in a boyhood between love
of breast and love again of breast,
    as ten will on the stage
    between you now, ten years
too old for Juliet and, in ten years,
ten years too young to play the Nurse.

*

Nothing dreadful ever happens in one
moment – each doubt's shadow needs
    an hour to fall. But sunlight
    fills a moment, hope twists
its baby hand around a moment, yes
consoles the moment. A year will sag,
    a marquee roof after the storm.
    A century thrills in showing off
its vile trophies, turns them in the light.
Terrific melancholy hogs an age.

The tinny night *is* my afternoon.
The sinking clouds are mostly rumour,
    twilight a puppet state I hear
    news from; the day's flamingo
embers are glitches I have by heart from
boyhood, to which I count back forty
    million backward steps, back –
    in sweet linen, sweeter cotton,
sweetest swaddling silk – to stay the calm.
Some day I'll lie beneath a colder cloth.

*

A wag who claps like a sealion when
he laughs; a fool who will not suffer
    fools; a rumbling tycoon;
    a monkey in a monkey suit:
those are not the parts I choose to play,
those gimping tennis racket parts.
    Give me the lad who springs
    to herohood on gala day; the man
maestro, and you playing my young bride
or my champion, or my young bride.

*

Each golden age gives way to thaw,
each thaw to months of spring, in
    squalor, counting copper,
    imagined bunts at the back
of the wine rack. The spice rack
dips to empties, a few dry sticks
    and stars, a flux of dill in oil.
    You hope for a hand of truffles,
each a thumb, a great knife anchored
in a ham, the pantomime bag of gold.

It's love I want, and the song which
follows love. The canny song of songs.
          Then the looking upwards
          and the cavalier inspection
of ceiling, skylight, sky. That's where
the lights should be, blaring on gantries.
          The looking upwards, where air is
          warmer, though I know my place
beneath the bed, where cool air drifts
and turns the dust of my former selves.

*

I cast you as the young countess, as
young Marie in *The Marie Curie Story*,
          as Bethany in *Stars Burn Gold*,
          as Gabriella in *The Marmoset*.
I think we'd talk of comets; your hand
on the bath's lip holds a flute or your
          hand smooths a length of rain
          from my cheek, your hand
thrusts up from the drifts of snow,
as once again we slip the avalanche.

*

Midnight means The Strand, the musk
of the dressing room still on me
          and still I fear the fearful
          impracticalities of the real:
the splintering of the Inspector's
pencil lead, the shadow of a stagehand
          crossing the soliloquy spot,
          the out-of-character sneezing
of the butler as he holds up his salver
of pink wafers and perfect sandwiches.

It's pay and play. Slip in a sixpence
and I'll dance and give the mob
     its thrills, say what they
     want me to. What's another
word for *mirador*? What's another
word for *wanion*? What might daint
     and sturd mean? Then calm
     as you appear in slouch clothes,
sliding a coin into the vending machine,
selecting Coffee – Black – No Sugar.

*

I dream I lose a tooth and sure enough,
that day, the tooth comes out. I dream
     a friend I haven't seen in years
     walks past me on The Strand
and that that evening, he does. I dream an
apple drops upon my head and though it
     takes two days that too turns true.
     Then I dream that all that
happens between us does not happen.
And we both know that will happen.

*

Hauled from one calm to another,
shocked by your shock of ringlets,
     slushed and tomfooled, I am
     an ape reaching through bars,
the leashed mongrel waiting, his nose
to the glass, while his master dips into
     the sweet shop, to stockpile gum
     and sherbets. No pay for silence
in this game; no call for mime troupes or
     gawping mummers, mouths sewn shut.

Blasphemy is minor bathroom tragedy –
a stubbed toe or a shaving nick and
   a mutter of *Lord God!* A rule
   is just a law with a grin.
You must step over, as you step over
the threshold of a year, aware the next
   will be the same but slower.
   As in the latest dream you walk
towards me from ten paces away
and with each step you age one year.

*

Some name it pain, this knowing
(whatever's meant by that). Some
   claim this undoing's just, this
   bolt of unluck sent from sense,
the path back cleared and well-lit, soft
to walk on (whatever's meant by that).
   I'll stand here in the stairwell now,
   learn my lesson, my lines, I mean.
Then I'll strut into the green room brim
with charm (whatever's meant by that).

*

Whatever your cutty costume leaves
to the imagination, I must imagine. Since
   the apparatus has no pattern,
   I can walk these seven aisles
of costumes when the stitchers leave
for wine bars then suburban rooms,
   and not be bussed or burned
   by ghosts. What sort of ageing,
choppy boy could not bite the head
from whatever thing most feared him?

If I could wrap myself around a ghost,
my heat might set alight its tablecloth,
        its ghouling shroud. A ghost
        is just a sanction for your fear
and fear desire's chilly twin. This far
inland, any dumb thing might combust
        for lack of moisture: gorse seeds
        hoisted in fire-climax, arsenic
sublimed. At the script's edge, I draw
myself, arms round the writhing ghost.

*

The wine bar singer's first song falls
far short of certain, the second song
        falls short of absolute.
        Catching a drift of the third,
aimless ruin leans over and flips
the volume up. The ceiling cracks –
        a crack the shape of the profile
        of someone lovely in profile
only. The stitchers smack their glasses
together, to stave off the gangling night.

*

In my notes my character is *stronger,
more insolent* yet I prefer to play him
        provident; his voice announces
        bounty – which regenerates
those boats which plough the tides
around your coast. An aquamariner
        drops anchor in a pool of sun;
        a cabin boy with a sickening
for you raises his flag of surrender,
surrender being simplest of all choices.

As one apparatus might beguile
its opposite, *seldom* and *often* form
        an awkward camaraderie,
        a cabaret-style double act.
My seldom pungency might court
my often thin, clear glaze of sorrows.
        I'd like you playing opposite me,
        some front row gazer saying,
She's ecstatic! and me knowing
whether that's implicit, or a guess.

*

Near midnight, The Embankment
and a fire blazing somewhere down
        the wharfs. Blood thumps
        and I think this city would
be nothing if I wasn't walking here
within its heart. A folly moment,
        moment of an upbeat dread.
        Even now, I'm one of thousands
walking and among them, the paragon,
the absolute and the shorn of shame.

*

Think of the palest pale blue – paler
than that is my colour. The sails of
        my yawl would be that shade;
        my blessing gown and shawl,
my winding sheet. And yet they make
me play the man in black, the man in
        grey and seldom the concession
        of a silky buttonhole or silver tie
and the only white allowed: my face
when faced with the burden of the truth.

All still. Though there, beneath the basin,
light barely creeps, though not dipping
   into the inappropriate, not
   at all like a girl skipping.
The audience pall in. I pull my pale,
damp legs into my character's stiff trousers,
   dip my head into the corridor,
   listen for voices in the stairwell,
check the great window for the glow
of the stage door light. Still there.

*

What's endless? Not the day which
hones and swoops and swallowtails
   down grey streets off The Strand,
   its splashdown marked by bells
and street to street-side hollering of names.
And I have heard yours mentioned now,
   completing the crescendo down
   from character to stage name
to swaddling name. Step up then, gowned
Amanda, now Francesca, now plain Ruth.

*

I run a bath for us – a daydream moment
soon regretted. What apparatus monitors
   the blood's impatience?
   What is best, appropriate?
My promise is to scour, to lock, to sweep,
to calibrate, to fumigate, to launder, daunt
   and sweat it out. My promise
   is to be seen, be seen to stand
on both sides of the scrim. Sleep next to
a cat and beasts will amble in your dream.

Yes, the night is a *no* thing. No, I mean
the night is a *yes* thing. Familiar, I mean:
    yawns between great buildings,
    half-paths through park grass,
night birds, once day birds, which roost
uneasy, could offer sirens, drill drones,
    alibis for silence, which lives on
    behind glass: in a booth, a dolly
sifts notes; in a gym window, a jowly
boxer is gunning fresh air: yes, no, yes.

*

The crested lark, the catkin yew,
the lugworm's cast: these I call to
    when someone begins a rant
    with 'In this game...' A tusk is not
an apparatus, nor is a trunk or jerking seed
pod. And if this is a game, I have not seen
    the rules – and a rule is just a law
    with doubts. We're in charge of
everything but hope. But hope, though
seldomtimes, winks in each direction.

*

Why? Because you offer moments
when all is lost – the whole path back
    forgotten, back story ripped
    and binned. I see you are
the sort to slip away, one large glass
and gone. Not that we would speak –
    I'm at another table rehearsing
    the smallest talk that goes for
currency, aftershow. I check the script:
no rewrites, no comeback, no slips.

The run must end. I will not call it
end if I can call it *compromise*.
      Everything but the harp, they
      say, and surely I have played
even the harp, or at least the thought
of it, drawing my fingers back toward
      the heart, to pluck the sad sound
      of your name and where it's gone;
the whine from a large glass; the last
whine from the beast below the floor.

*

When at last we see a ghost and he
is not a he, but a slim, brown leaf
      or a cloth acting in a way a leaf
      or cloth could not: pulsed
behind a window or levitated, then
fear arrives softly, wavelets on sand.
      The ghost we imagine equals
      the terror within us. The you
I imagine is seldom the you that I get.
Compromise is sturdier than love.

*

As daisies, a dearth of them this year,
jig in the Embankment Gardens,
      I realise that the apparatus
      and the apparition are the same,
or appear to be. The ghost who pushes
past you in the stairwell has familiar gait
      as he turns again down the stair,
      down all the steps back and back.
The last step on the stair is the darkest.
When one door closes another door shuts.

Six Ripple Poems

Relics

Syd Barrett (1946-2006)

Memories rose – hints of pink: corals,
carbolics, bubblegums; bop, soul, rock,
progressive, each lick of production slicker,
the suites more gunned with haze, the suits slacker.

Electrics snarl, the circuit's shaky circle
unwheeling, madcapped, the air brim with colours,
nursery songs, the Heath-Robinsonian organ's sacral
wheeze, *forever and ever*, the drifting carousel.

Spiral

These years lift over coldly now: Aprils
and Augusts are gifted to ice, or sprawl
into mid-summers or year ends – pillars
of lesser standing. Still come no replies

to boyish queries, how the belly sleeper
buoys, begins again, becomes poor soul
or bull of appetite; why when the pearls
drop, no spool dares connect the ripples.

Eidolon

Down in fame's flood, down an alley, down-
wind of now, elegant in self-denial,
an Iron Range wraith junking cue cards, an ideal,
an idol before which the zeitgeist kneeled.

Dylan, named for a poet named for an old
tale of the child who crawled to the sea, this land
is yours: the black plain the needle
ploughs from lip to label; be all, end all.

Losses
Percy Shaw (1890-1976)

Candida spores, heads of sweet cicely,
stars of the least magnitude, flicker of souls
in graveyard photographs, brief ands and alsos
flipping in the small talk, we see less

and less each year, dark driving; the mind seals
its terminal deal with blackness, sells
the silver, pawns the phosphene; timelines slice
from dot to dot: caviar, clove-pegs, sloes.

Sailor

Arthur Russell (1951-1992)

Though one eternal argument is as real
as the next one – plasma in a solar
wind of change or lack of change, a reversal
of instinctive swerving, switch of roles –

he'd solve this code, rip through the scroll of rules
(though read them first), intent to sail or see
that backbeat in the distant sky, a pulsar
spinning in its orbis of arousal.

Schema

Make a bet on what will rise, will scum
up in the process, what will succumb
to surfacing, or settling when the mix
begins to slow. Stare through the chasm,

most orange or most blue, which comes
to revel in dire standstill, this tinted musk
of tinctured clarity which somehow makes
a feature of your dazzled, O-mouthed mask.

STEADY GRINDING BLUES

Alembic Finger Count

San Francisco

Night comes Kampala quick, Quito quick,
kids drift, but quick, off Golden Gate Park
into a burger church or a family car the size
of a nun's chapel. Now the older ones huddle
in personae vitae, leaning in with beer
clutched in brown bags – Pabst, Tecate, Bud.

In the Haight's first chic dive, tonight's
specials are sweetbreads and honeycomb tripe.
Filaments hang in bulbs along the bar,
smarting my eyes, but spraying as little light
as the self-immolating sprites they resemble –
just enough to count my fingers in the dim.

The barman exudes imperial scuzz, it takes him
an hour to muss that doorway hobo hair.

Chinatown Funeral Motorcade

San Francisco

Did you think to speak of your own life, traveller?

As with the flies on this watermelon rind,
I misrelish to eat alone though, never keen
to eat in company, true, mostly I don't care to eat.

The miso rises in the soup –
pelagic lava in an early hours undersea documentary
rerun. Quite soon, they'll be cremating that man
whose parade I stumbled on... I push my chopsticks
into the sticky rice beneath the katsu, so I can
get this down but, seeing I have made
the symbol of death, I resettle them on the bowl's lip.

On the kitty-corner of Broadway and Powell,
the naval band, as many pale faces
as I'd seen in tandem all week, blew forth
some melancholy air – a maritime *piobaireachd* –
and while the conductress thrummed a gong
mourners bore a bouqueted likeness of the dead one;
the hatted driver of the hearse flipped wads
of fake bills – an anti-scramble.
The lucky cat
holds his paw in its perennial wave of *maybe*,
perhaps; the proprietress knocks in a bracket,
re-hangs a floral still life – more follower
of Fantin-Latour than Shunboku.
I am thinking
of those trumpeters and trombonists, scrappy hair
bound into Sunday-duty ponytails, caps underarm,
heading down Powell to catch the last of the game
and I *their* follower for a few blocks north
towards the Bay, to this pan-Asian coffee house,

where I write these lines,
aged forty three and four months, a limited achiever,
the drift of a sad song never far from my head.
There is hyperreality, there is the promise of rain.
Guest Check Number 09224 – $13.14.

Hazy Alley Incident

Eugene, OR

Girl shouting *Oliver!* at the top of the cut-through
by Jacob's Gallery, you have now entered
the slenderest of histories, the skin-bound book
I store between my temples; in that mean
and moonless city, you must hang fraught
in your too-long coat, not a winner, but placed,
and in this cutty version of forever, forever
calling on your unseen beau, one flake in
a limbic blizzard, one spark in the synaptic blaze.
And now the rain turns, light but going steady
on the Willamette. Along the bank, I lift my pace
from *devil-may-have-me to heading somewhere*
and still your mouth in the haze calling is
a ruby carbuncle woken by a miner's head-beam,
the reddest berry in the hedgerow, which all
but the bird in the fable know not to pluck.

Freight Train Interlude

Eugene, OR

Roseberg   Roseberg   Roseberg   Roseberg
Wherever this timber is launched toward, Mr
Roseberg, I presume you'd brighten, knowing
this half-mile box-car train has stopped the
traffic and that citizens fold arms at crossings,
some patient, some frustrated, and only I am
having for the first time the old 'shall I jump
into one empty car' thrill, except I know it is
the boy in me who wants it, not the fool-like
travelling moper, chewing the glass of his
many irks, roasting the bones of his fewer
thoughts, westering in drizzle and casualwear,
who waits for the all-clear bell to ring, for the
town centre to usher him back; the Inuit does
not leap into the hole he cuts in the ice; the
locals on Princes Street do not gawp up at the
Castle; that which is in the sea does not know
that it tastes of the sea; I *am* the man they
think I am and I *am* the man I used to be.
Roseberg   Roseberg   Roseberg   Roseberg

Holiday Melisma Overdub

Eugene, OR

> *Happy happy is*
> *the man who knows this:*
> *a woman who can sing*
> *is everything.*

ANON

A moth is essentially a lever, alive and breathing,
its fulcrum like a switch deep in the brain,
and I was mulling over whether a lever

is my favourite machine when a voice tugged
the stud of recognition: familiar – 'unmistakeable'
as some duff, dread vinylist would have it –

but *treated* I'd swear; the big bands
were not *that* big, not then, when people dived
for smoothness since they so wanted smoothness.

Billie buffed up, sounding drip-fed: beef tea,
treacle, corporate unction; Billie spilling
from the awnings of a seafood restaurant,

a yard-end stream sweetening the morning.
I wheel my suitcase into Cornucopia, where
my soup and sandwich earn their serenade,

a reggae cover of 'Time' which plays through twice.
It's too early for $1 Pinnacle Flavor Kamikaze
Shots, too late for my knee-bandaged neighbour

who is scuttling her second Bloody Mary, too late
for the ancient maidens dunking into salads bigger
than their jolly roger heads. Time is the *mastah – eh!*

And as I look up – retiring after fifty-five years,
the TV pundit concludes, 'Baseball is cigar smoke,
Ladies' Day, down in front,' and such enigmas

settle me – warm milk on an empty stomach.
Just then, I feel I might explain ball lightning,
skyquake, déjà vu, hone the square root of minus one,

but Billie is guesswork, vita brevis, singing on
in all these towns with streets named for trees,
dubbed into the mind's hive, her honey face

a decal on the nation's arm. Look, it's turned noon –
day-flying moths are moving the earth,
the sidewalks are strewn with windfalls.

Puget Sound Piece

Seattle

(lacrimoso)

Ever heard a song that made you cry?
And where were you anyway?

I was noticing how, beyond the mountains,
there are taller mountains, thinking that it's good to be
in a city of perspectives after a three day mope,
and that this place reminds me of Lisbon.

And right enough, here's a Mexican stroller
trying an edge-of-town lament that's just a back-alley slap
away from fado, just as *lynxish*, as *maigre*.
I hobble on; the sun brings up my grey, rests
here on my paunch, as a baby's head does not.

An Arcadian cover of 'Like a Prayer' is sweeter
than the tour-trek snores of Bad Brains with whom
I shared a train car from Portland yesterday.
A blue collar crooner yaws 'The Star-Spangled Banner'
on the corner of the fruit and fish markets
where the smell – the accusation – swings
from peach to crab and the sellers talk up
limb-length salmon and lobsters: *Rolls-Royce of the Sea*.

Accusations swing, just as my gout-flared dreams
are imped by rue and reprimand: pill-sick,
I've barely eaten in a week, as muddy pink
as the boy at the market's end who offers
some white boy Wonder. Then 'Enter Sandman'
yaps from the city's oldest saloon, a seahawk
descends the skyscape of the barmaid's neck.

I look thirty in the gantry mirror. I think.
When we load the well with noise – the squalor
of wiry laughter, cries of soon snuffed triumph,

soon repeated pain – we revive damnation. I think
of that vixen cub who came to me at the Court corner,
the treasure wet of her nose on my knuckles,
her brief mew a sad song new in my repertoire.

A fox tilts its sniff at you twice: first
for your scent, then to establish if you contain water
which, as we so often prove, we do.

Highway Forgiving Song

King George Highway, BC

As love crawls across great faults,
the bullfinch strives along the path
of power lines, the pickers thread
up stubby crop lines, the cherry-engined
freight train drawls through an umpteenth county.

As the wilting heart renews, renews,
the foal stands quick beside her dam,
the copter returns man to the air, which
once he fawned on and commanded, and
the mole revives the doldrum soil, a compact past.

As in dreams we hold past lovers
who have lived on half-heartedly, and tell
us so, these coach wheels hold the road
in brief but constant purchase, the creek
holds course, sees through its downbeat drama

and in the dreamt embrace, we say *I know, I know.*

Convict Julie Catachresis

Vancouver

By turns, a man softens, his neighbour tips
a cap at his douce face as he moves
around the lawn, a two hour job, but his dreams
remind him he was quick and cruel.

One drowses in slacks at the bus stop
encouraging surprises:
an undiscovered bar on a cross street
or a twenty folded small in a back pocket.

Another pushes his errand cart
across Commercial Drive, his Calabrian face –
once falcon and now sparrow –
has blanched, as has the rotten past.

In the aquarium, near blind and scything,
a black knifefish feeds by electrical pulses,
a puffer blows through sand
contented by oblivious, almost hope.

In one tank, the cichlids move on
at stagnant pace, except for
the convict julies, which dart and harass,
named for their jail garb stripes.

I'm not in this; numb to such attrition,
I'm the side of the coin with a face
not a sword, an empty hand that mimes
the shapes of missing things.

Still in that room. The day for games
is done, the dusk bus winks over
a middle distance hill. Streets clear, bars
shutter up, fishtanks are flicked into abyssal dark

where the little convicts shuffle,
unmoved by our insinuative naming,
abuse. There is never a path back
and each Monday will contain *that* Monday

or each Friday evening
flaunt the taint of its black thought
and such is allegiance
that the wilting boxers cling,

close to love, or trusted enemies
lean nearer, eyeing shyly; a spring
works loose in the depths of the machine.
Still in that room. *Still in that room.*

Water Street Drop-off

James Merrill House, Stonington, CT

Long sleepless room, roof sloping. Willing
to fall under, I measure: to floorboard, one hand, to ceiling,

one foot; windows on four sides – parallel retort;
aching, gape-eyed, half below, ghost-start

throws front lobe halfway back from the precipice
of anima, my inner ceremony, glisk

of imagined marriage, past life, kismet:
wraith crews row boats of chaos through it;

exact pain tombstoning from temple
to jaw; sea lights are moochers: red apple, green apple;

the bitching half-dark taunts, the sly hack
of a week-long cough, bloodless, tart – shock

to the neck, thoughtless, to this unclassical torso;
a dismal oblong, the writer's piano

rehearses stasis; one moment of zenith touch
but in the next I long to pull the switch,

cast blackout in this not near empty vessel,
selfless mortar scoured by selfish pestle;

face down, near happy, cold coiled, fizzing;
hindsight waves its one colour flag, busy

systems catch, gut gurns, wishing well,
drencher, freshet, fever, storm port roll

down crawlspace, priest hole, panic room, oubliette;
COUGH *lightweight* COUGH *lighthouse* COUGH *regret*

COUGH *not much of a man* – enough of this –
tug up the comforter, engaging bliss,

donate the hustling brain as a grimoire
in which the small hours screed their black memoir.

Hallowe'en Downpour Downer

Manhattan

I have not known – though I have considered –
a middle order stag drifting miles north
and east through the greenwoods
not quite as I shift, ochlophobic,
from West Village to Lower East Side,
slow in this mid-evening rain, doused within

the moment's ecology, sifting a cold thought
in a corsair-houred, split melon night
and missing the motley friends
I'm unsure *are* friends, woeing,
not tallying what could happen at the
limits of what could happen if the city flicked

a dream light on, were a salty redheaded thought
to push through the costumed crowds
and level with me, levelling me
with its stiff slap, begging me,
where can we ever be alone, oh when
can we start to sing the steady grinding blues?